CULT OF THE HARLEY-DAVIDSON

CULT OF THE HARLEY-DAVIDSON

AMERICA'S MOTORCYCLE HERITAGE IN COLOUR

HARLEY-DAVIDSON
MOTOR CO. INC.

GERALD FOSTER

Osprey Colour Series

First published in autumn 1982 by
Osprey Publishing Limited
12-14 Long Acre, London WC2E 9LP
Reprinted winter 1982

British Library Cataloguing in Publication Data

Foster, Gerald
    Cult of the Harley-Davidson
    1. Harley-Davidson motorcycle—History
    I. Title
    629.2'275   TL448.H3

ISBN 0-85045-463-8

Editor Tim Parker

Printed in Hong Kong

There's no explaining the cult of the Harley-Davidson motorcycle. It's a worldwide phenomenon. Perhaps the photographs shown within go some way. Those who are part of that cult will know anyway, those who aren't might find some indication from the words below.

All the photographs were all taken in North America by Gerald Foster. Most were shot in California. All who needed to be participants in the taking of the shots were willing and enthusiastic. Those who were left out should not be offended—we could have quadrupled the content with ease. Harleys are ridden by police patrolmen, Hell's Angels, drag racers, flat trackers, regular weekenders, Sportsters, Supergliders, Electragliders and little old ladies in pink.

A Harley engine can always be rebuilt one more time . . . Mechanic

Harley parts are last in and first out, as opposed to Japanese shit which is first in and last out . . . Motorcycle used parts dealer

Contrary to popular belief, Harley riders do not work on their machines with a hammer and a hand grenade. Hand grenades are just too hard to come by these days. . .

I don't know man, it must be the mystic of the thing or something, but I ain't never seen an ugly looking chick on the back of a Harley . . . Imported bike rider

A lot of people sure don't like us, but I've seen that look which says 'I wish I was you' a thousand times when I pull up alongside a car at a red light. Running free on a Harley, there's nothing like it . . .

Hot dudes, hot mammas, hot steel

Gerald Foster has been associated with motorcycles for much of his life—as a competitor, designer, journalist and author (and now photographer). While he remained unconvinced that his photograph should appear on this page, he did agree to one somewhere in the book, provided the page wasn't mentioned.

His thanks must go to; Oliver of H-D Glendale, Neil's Silk Screen, Dave Kelly of Coco, Chubbock's Pasedena H-D, Ken Clapp and Bob Barkhimer Associates, the Harley-Davidson Motor Company and Bob Klein, and all the wonderful Harley-Davidson people who made this book possible. Special thanks, and they'll know why, must also go to Psycho, Bonnie (love ya babe!), Samantha and the lovely Anita.
The editor's thanks must go to the H-D rider he met with John Hall in a Westminster, California dealership for the seeds of this idea, to the Soho newsagent who informs him of what's selling this week, to Rich McCormack and Paul Pfanner for their serious approach, and to Kass and Mandy who tolerated more than they know.

This book is dedicated to the much maligned Harley-Davidson rider, who often seems to find the freedom the rest of us only dream about.

CONTENTS

HARLEY-DAVIDSON IS...

. . . a spring day at the races with friends

. . . a better than new 1970 Electraglide . . .

... and paying six grand and change for it

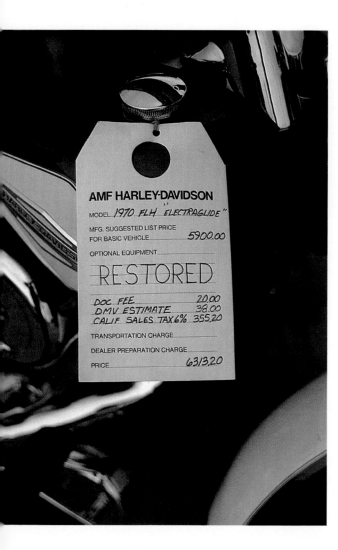

AMF HARLEY-DAVIDSON

MODEL *1970 FLH "ELECTRAGLIDE"*

MFG. SUGGESTED LIST PRICE
FOR BASIC VEHICLE...... *5900.00*

OPTIONAL EQUIPMENT......

RESTORED

DOC FEE   *20.00*
DMV ESTIMATE   *38.00*
CALIF. SALES TAX 6% *355.20*

TRANSPORTATION CHARGE......

DEALER PREPARATION CHARGE......

PRICE...... *6313.20*

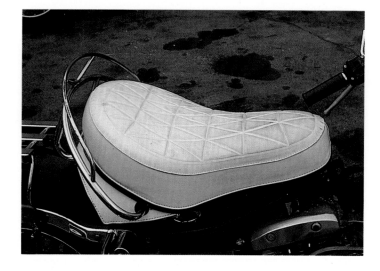

... a comfortable seat for long rides

. . . the last overnight get together of the year

. . . a two-stroke golf cart (**below**)

. . . a no longer in production XLCR café racer

. . . $14.95 plus tax (**right**)

Insist on
Genuine

MOTOR
HARLEY-DAVIDSON
CYCLES

Parts and
Accessories

. . . metalflake fuel tank

. . . the belt drive making a comeback on the Sturgis

HARLEY-DAVIDSON AND THE LAW

Left As the Japanese make deeper inroads into what was once the sole preserve of the Milwaukee company—supplying motorcycles to the police forces of America—it is becoming increasingly difficult to find the big twins on the streets. This one was spotted by chance in beautiful downtown Burbank, California. Razor sharp creases in shirts, boots shined to a mirror finish, and the inevitable 'shades'. Sergeant Don Brown typifies the pride motorcycle patrolmen take in their appearance

Above Harley-Davidson advertising

HARLEY-DAVIDSON AND THE VICTOR MCLAGLEN MOTOR CORPS

Left Formed in 1935, the Victor McLaglen stunt and drill team takes its name from the academy award winning movie star who promoted the group. Purely as a hobby the group, all Harley mounted, regularly appears at shows and parades throughout the west. Ages of the group range from mid-twenties to several in their fifties

Below Personalised plate

HARLEY-DAVIDSON RIDERS FOR OTHERS

Left Much has been said and written about so called 'bikers', most of it disparaging. What is not picked up on is the amount bikers have done, and continue to do for a number of charities. Each year, for example, clubs and associations across the country organise 'toy runs' around Christmas time to provide toys for under privileged youngsters. The Salvation Army who distributes the toys, was very appreciative of this mountain at the Los Angeles toy run

Right Miss Piggy is an ongoing favorite at toy runs

Toy run day is also a place to meet old friends and look at other bikes . . .

Below The crippling disease, muscular dystrophy, is also a candidate for extinction if the Bikers of America have their way

MDA The Bikers of America are taking on the fight against Muscular Dystrophy. And we need you on our side. Muscular Dystrophy is a disease with no known cure. The way it is now, many kids who should grow up to ride—won't. But you have a chance to help change that, by joining in the "Bikers of America" fight against MD.

There will be fund-raising rallies, runs, parades, ride-ins, and other events all across America that you can participate in.

For details, see your local Harley-Davidson® dealer, or write "Bikers of America Fight MD," P. O. Box 653, Milwaukee, Wisc. 53201. We'll send you information on how you or your club can get involved

Come on out and join the fight against MD. It's a good cause, a good way to do something positive for your community and for motorcycling. And it's a great way to have some fun.

Biker Presents FTW November 1981

HARLEY-DAVIDSON AND THE ROCK STORE

The Rock Store, a rural grocery store and gas station in the Santa Monica mountains, thirty five miles west of downtown Los Angeles, is the Sunday meeting place for hundreds of motorcyclists to look, be seen, talk and generally take it easy in the California sunshine

27

Naturally, there is fierce brand loyalty but at the Rock Store, Harleys and Hondas, Ducatis and Kawasakis park next to one another. This one's all the way from Montreal, Canada

The Rock Store is together . . . or alone

Back to the city

MORE HARLEY-DAVIDSON IS...

. . . a welded chrome wheel by Invader

. . . a custom shop

. . . still available foot boards

. . . telling the world what you think **(left)**

. . . embroidered patches inside a glass case for safety **(above)**

. . . 'It's got your AM and FM. Your cassette
player. Your quartz clock. Your oil pressure
gauge. Your gas gauge. Your volt meter. And,
of course, your cigarette lighter'

. . . hundreds of dollars worth of chrome
(right)

. . . the Latin look

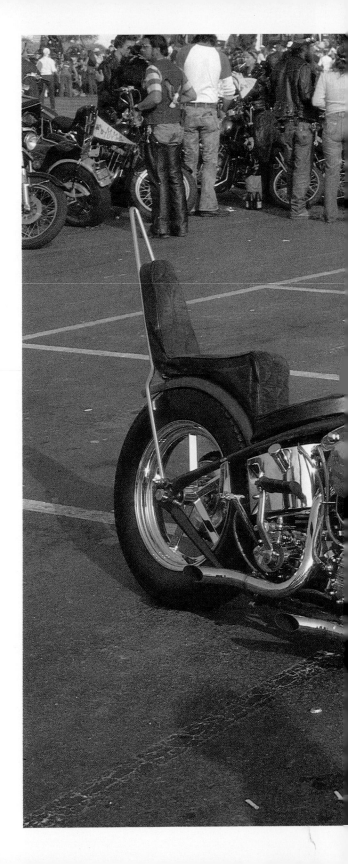

. . . a 1937 poster **(left)**

. . . family clubs

. . . a neat looking chopper **(following page)**

. . . turbo power **(left)**

. . . making friends even if it took the excuse
of a photograph to get you together **(above)**

HARLEY-DAVIDSON AND THE BUSINESS WORLD

Tom Rudd, a former motorcycle drag racer of Minneapolis, Minnesota, started a fledgling company fourteen years ago to sell performance products he developed. Today Rudd is a millionaire. His company, Drag Specialties, is the largest aftermarket supplier of motorcycle parts and accessories in the world

HARLEY-DAVIDSON AND THEIR DEALERS

The plant is built on the site of the first factory —a ten by fifteen foot wooden building in the Davidson's back yard

Mecca **(below)**

Marina Del Rey, California **(below)**   The service department **(right)**

THE dealership

Harleys never die. Proud of its comfort and
overhead valves **(below)**

San Gabriel Valley, California **(right)**

HARLEY-DAVIDSON SIDECARS AND TRIKES

Below Long a favorite of the parking ticket lady, the Servicar is being phased out in favor of the more 'energy efficient' Cushman. Luckily, most trikes sold off by police departments find good homes. During forty years of continued manufacture the Servicar was powered by the 45 cu.in. side valve twin. Though she is as effective—note the ticket on the windshield—the Cushman somehow doesn't seem so imposing
Right The customised license plate gives the year

Yes, it is hers

Following page Not a sidecar, nor a trike:
instead an Electraglide and trailer. No horses,
just picnic lunch

'Half Rat' is an immaculately re-engineered
'45

Something for the family man

HARLEY-DAVIDSON AND THE KING OF THE CUSTOMISERS

Left No man has influenced American motorcycle styling more than Arlen Ness; his original 'Bay Area Low Rider' became the basis of a style followed by many, including the Harley-Davidson factory. In less than a dozen years Ness has established himself as an innovator and builder without equal. It was probably only natural that the king of the customisers wouldn't be satisfied with an ordinary van; the roofline of this one is considerably lower than the production version

Below All Ness' bikes have names. This one —the Tattoo bike—needs little explaining

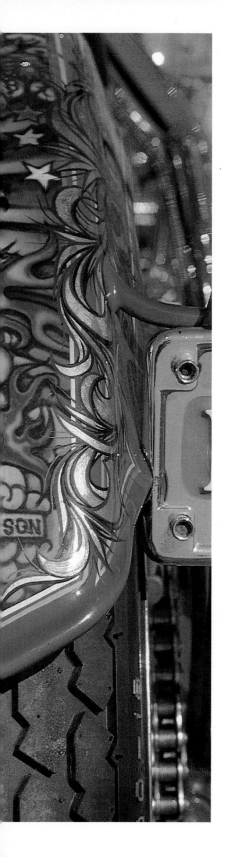

Ness-tique

Indian style **(right)**

Untouchable **(following page)**

Engraving and gold plating turn motorcycles
into works of art

A silver and gold—with diamonds in the pedal bearings—replica of Harley-Davidson's first motorcycle. One of the only three in existence, (maybe to match the number of motorcycles manufactured), the machine was won by Ness at the 1979 Daytona Custom Show

HARLEY-DAVIDSON AND RACING

Flat Track Racing

Left The dominant force in American dirt track racing—Jay Springsteen and Harley-Davidson. Jay captured his first AMA title in 1976 on a factory XR750, and two more in '77 and '78

Below The XR750 engine—nothing exotic, just years and years of painstaking development

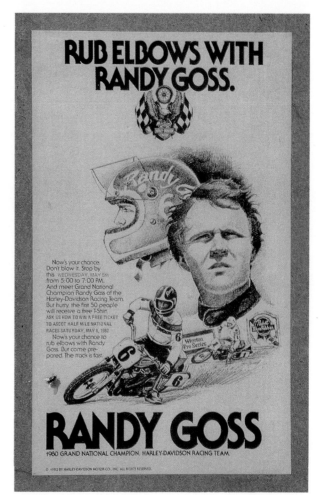

Above Meet the stars, check out our bikes. Harley-Davidson has evolved a unique advertising campaign whereby their factory riders visit dealerships between races

Left The XR750 is capable of 130 plus miles an hour on mile dirt tracks

Following page Scott Pearson gets the hole shot on the ultrafast San Jose mile track

Steve Eklund (8) leads Ted Boody

Drag Racing

Keith Ruxon aboard his top fuel burning
dragster

If we advance the timing . . .

Nitro burner **(below)**

Immaculately prepared drag bikes are the
rule rather than the exception **(right)**

Staged

Built for the Bonneville Salt Flats

Kenny Lyons took three years to complete his dream—a V4 Turbo charged 150 cu.in. Bonneville Harley-Davidson racer. Not just two engines bolted side by side but a complete design from the new four hole crankcases up

HARLEY-DAVIDSON AND THE ESCORT RIDER

Below Escorting funeral processions along the crowded streets and freeways of Southern California is work to Harry Fisher, owner of the V.I.P. motorcycle escort service in Bellflower

Above 'I can handle up to 15 cars alone in quieter parts of the city,' says Fisher, 'but with all the traffic in Hollywood I need another rider for more than ten'

Left Providing he enters an intersection on green, Fisher can hold cross traffic (even if the light turns red) while the procession speeds through. With traffic signals at seemingly every intersection the Harley-Davidson spends its time either at idle or accelerating to catch up with the procession

HARLEY-DAVIDSON PAST AND PRESENT

Left A 1911 Silent Gray Fellow. The origin of the nickname was due to Harley-Davidson successfully muffling the exhaust noise, the all gray standard paint job, and the almost human companionship the machine offered the rider

Below A 1926 'Peashooter' racer

Left 1929 saw the introduction of the WL 45 sidevalve twin, a design which endured thru '51 in two wheelers and '73 in the three wheeled Servicars

Below 1930 was the first year of the popular 74 in. sidevalve VL model

The first overhead valve twin—the 61 cu.in.
EL model—was the first Harley to use a
circulatory oil system

Left The 61 cu.in. EL came to be known as the 'Knucklehead'

Below The 45 and 55 inch K and KH models which superseded the WL in 1952 were the forerunners of the Sportster

Introduced in 1957 the Sportster is currently
celebrating twenty five years of production

The 'Panhead', with hydraulic lifters and
aluminium heads came into being in 1948

Dennis Doland with his beautifully restored
'56 'Panhead'

The 'Shovelhead' introduced in the mid-sixties
is the current big twin Harley engine

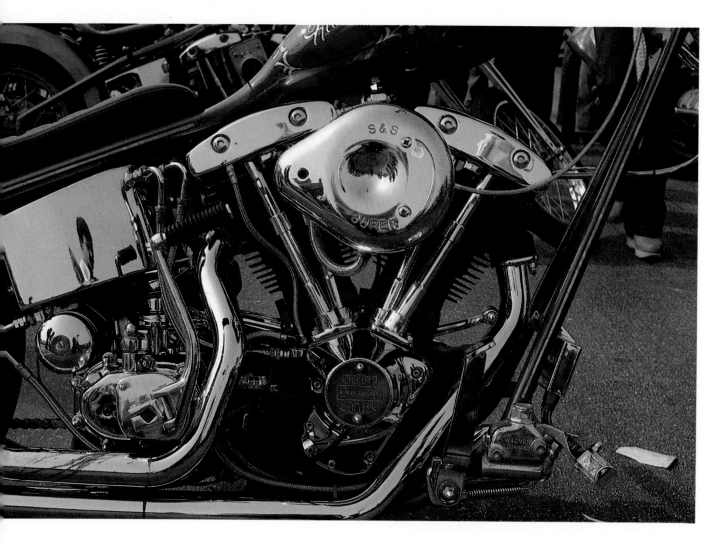

More custom 'Shovelhead' in gold and chrome

HARLEY-DAVIDSON AND THE ALTERNATIVE LIFESTYLE

Marriage

Terry and Renee LIVE Harley-Davidson, so it seemed natural for bikes to be in attendance at their outdoor wedding

Leaving for the reception **(right)**

Motorcycle clubs

Left To many, the image of the motorcycle club is somewhat akin to that of a band of outlaws. And, while they might project an image which tends to intimidate, in general the opposite is true. The Fifth Chapter is such a club, but there is more to this group than meets the eye. Serious drinking and drug problems bring them together; a love of motorcycles and riding provides the binding thread to sobriety

Right The Los Angeles Fifth Chapter—a portrait

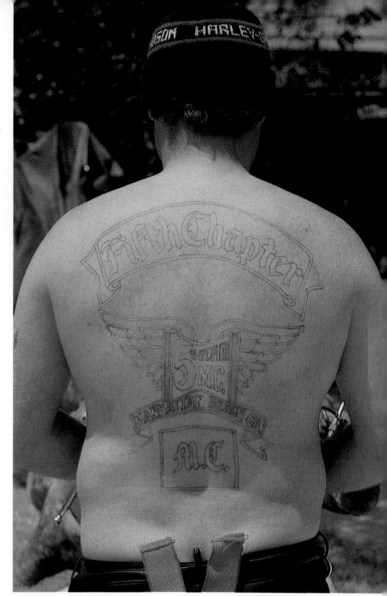

Above The commitment here is much more than skin deep

Following page Club run

Rat bikes

No one seems to know how or why the Rat Bike evolved. But don't be fooled, these wired together oil covered beauties give good account of themselves, and will probably still be running strong when everything else is long gone

Tattoos

In addition to the Cistine Chapel, some of the finest art in the world is found on bodies

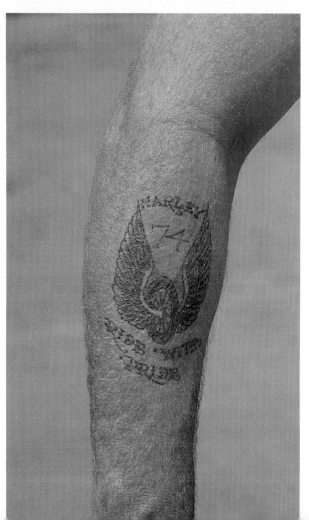

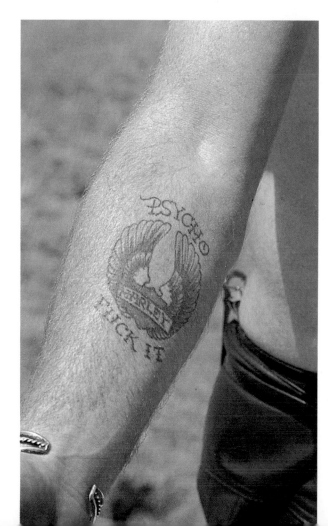

Beards

Beards and Harley-Davidson go together like baseball and hotdogs

T shirts and things

Bunnie's answer to the inevitable biker request, 'Show us your . . .'. **(far left)** Anita **(left)**

Hawg power

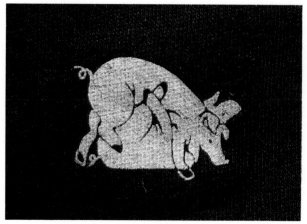

My Ol' Lady Yes,
My Dog Maybe,
My
Harley–Davidson
NEVER.

Frobe **(right)**
Melissa Moviestar **(left)**

Last picture in the book, but one

Below In June, 1981, The Harley-Davidson Motor Company returned to private ownership when the company was purchased from the American Machine & Foundry Company. The legend lives on

Legend in the making?